Beyond the Self

Beyond the Self

TEACHINGS ON THE MIDDLE WAY

Thich Nhat Hanh

PARALLAX PRESS
BERKELEY, CALIFORNIA

PARALLAX PRESS
P.O. Box 7355
Berkeley, California 94707
www.parallax.org

Parallax Press is the publishing division
of Unified Buddhist Church, Inc.

Printed in the United States of America.

Cover and text design by Jess Morphew.
Author photo by Richard Friday.

The sutra translated here is Number 301 in the Samyukta Agama; the Samyukta Agama is Number 29 in the Chinese canon. The equivalent sutra in Pali is the Kaccayanagotta Sutta, Samyutta Nikaya 12.15.

Library of Congress Cataloging-in-Publication Data
Nhât Hanh, Thích.
Beyond the self : teachings on the middle way / Thich Nhat Hanh.
p. cm.
ISBN 978-1-935209-41-6
1. Madhyamika (Buddhism) I. Title.
BQ9800.T5392N45427 2010
294.3'92--dc22

2009039699

1 2 3 4 5 / 14 13 12 11 10

Contents

Introduction

The morning of the Buddha's enlightenment at the foot of the bodhi tree, he was so surprised. He had been meditating for the whole night. In the early morning, at the moment when he saw the morning star, he declared, "How strange! Everyone has the capacity to be awake, to understand, and to love. Yet they continue to drift and sink on the ocean of suffering, life after life."

Before he became the Buddha, "the awakened one," Prince Siddhartha had a strong will to succeed. He tried to use his mind to suppress his mind and body, putting himself through a period of practicing self-mortification and extreme austerity in which he almost died. Eventually, he accepted that forcing his body and mind in the practice wouldn't help him, so he adopted the Middle Way, a path between austerity and indulgence in sensual pleasure.

Soon after Siddhartha woke up and became the Buddha, he wanted to share what he had learned. His first Dharma talk was offered to the five co-practitioners who had practiced asceticism with him.

He said, "My brothers, there are two extremes that a person on the path should avoid. One is to indulge in sensual pleasures, and the other is to practice austerities that deprive the body of its needs. Both of these extremes lead to failure. The path I have discovered is the Middle Way, which avoids both extremes and has the capacity to lead one to understanding, liberation, and peace. It is the Noble Eightfold Path of Right View, Right Thought, Right Speech, Right Action, Right Livelihood, Right Effort, Right Mindfulness, and Right Concentration. I have followed this Noble Eightfold Path and have realized understanding, liberation, and peace. Brothers, why do I call this path the right path? I call it the right path because it does not avoid or deny suffering, but allows for a direct confrontation with suffering as the means to overcome it. The Noble Eightfold Path is the path of living in awareness."

From his very first Dharma talk, the Buddha spoke about the Middle Way, the Four Noble Truths, and the Noble Eightfold Path. He continued to teach on these subjects throughout his life.

When the Buddha appeared in the world, he was a great revolutionary. He taught that everything is impermanent and subject to change and that what we call "self" or "self-nature" doesn't exist. The Buddha's teaching of no-self was in direct contradiction to the philosophy and religion prevalent in India at the time, and it generated a strong reaction. Hinduism believes that each of us has a divine self (*atman*) that is eternal and is part of the great divine self (*brahman*).

When the Buddha was still alive, his teachings were clear and powerful. After the Buddha's death, the Buddha's disciples had to develop their own teachings to respond to the continued opposition from Hinduism. Sometimes they brought up new theories that were far from the original teachings of the Buddha. There was much back and forth as Hindu scholars and scholars from the various schools of Buddhism contradicted and challenged each other. In the second century, the Buddhist scholar Nagarjuna wrote the Madhyamaka Shastra, a commentary of the Buddha's teachings on the Middle Way, in an effort to return to and clarify the Buddha's original meaning.

The Sutra on the Middle Way contains the key Buddhist concepts of Right View: keeping an open mind and avoiding extreme perspectives and dualities, and Dependent Co-arising: the interdependent, mutually-created nature of all things.

The sutra uses the term "Right View" to mean a view that transcends dualistic thinking and is not caught in worldly views. Worldly views, views based on the surface appearance of things, are fetters.

In the Diamond Sutra, the Buddha talks about four notions that affect all our views and perceptions. These four notions need to be thrown away.

The first notion we need to throw away is the notion of self. There is the idea that I am this body, this body is me or, this body is mine and it belongs to me. We say these things based on the notion that "I am." But a better statement would be, "I inter-am." It's closer to the truth in the light of interconnectedness; we see there is no separate self that can exist by itself. You cannot exist without your parents, your ancestors, food, water, air, earth, and everything else in the cosmos. By looking deeply into the nature of reality, we can throw away the notion "I am."

The second notion the Diamond Sutra advises us to throw away is the notion of person or human being. When we look into the human being, we see animal ancestors, we see plant and mineral ancestors. A human is made of non-human elements. If we take away the non-human elements, the human being would no longer be there. This is the oldest teaching on deep ecology. In order to protect the human being, you have to protect what is not human. Discriminating between human and nature is a wrong view.

The third wrong notion is that of living beings.

We distinguish living beings from non-living beings. We distinguish humans and animals from plants and minerals. But looking deeply into living beings, we see elements that we call non-living beings: plants and minerals. You can see that plants and minerals are also alive. After meditation we see there's no real frontier separating living beings and so-called non-living beings.

The fourth notion to be thrown away is the notion of life span. We believe that we're born at one point in time, that we shall die at another point in time, and that in between is our life span. Most of us believe we'll spend seventy, eighty, ninety, one hundred years on this planet and then we'll be gone. But when we look deeply, we see this is a wrong perception. In our mind, to be born means that from nothing we become something, to die means that from something we become nothing; and from someone we become no one. But a cloud can't be born; it has come from the water in the rivers and oceans, and dust and the heat of the sun have helped create it. A cloud can never die; it can only become rain or snow. A piece of paper can't be born; it's made of trees, the sun, the cloud, the logger, and the worker in the paper factory. When we burn a piece of paper, the paper is transformed into heat, ash, and smoke; it cannot be reduced to nothingness. Birth and death are notions that cannot be applied to reality.

These four notions are at the foundation of our fear, discrimination, and suffering. When we are able to see them as wrong views, ignorance and suffering will no longer touch us. We'll no longer suffer because of our wrong views.

When we are caught in ideas of self, human being, living being, or life span, it's because we haven't been able to see Dependent Co-arising. When we are caught in the idea of a life span, we think, my life will only last a certain amount of time, and we start asking questions like, "Did I exist in the past?" "What was I in the past?" "When I die, will I still be there, and if I am, what will I be?" These questions only arise when we are caught in the ideas of self, human being, living being, and life span.

The Sanskrit phrase *pratitya samutpada* means "in dependence, things rise up." Pratitya samutpada is sometimes called the teaching of cause and effect. But that can be misleading, because we usually think of cause and effect as separate entities, with cause always preceding effect, and one cause leading to one effect. According to the teaching of Dependent Co-arising, cause and effect arise together (samutpada) and everything is a result of multiple causes and conditions.

For a table to exist, we need wood, a carpenter,

time, skillfulness, and many other causes. And each of these causes needs other causes in order to be. The wood needs the forest, the sunshine, the rain, and so on. The carpenter needs his parents, breakfast, fresh air, and so on. And each of these things, in turn, has to be brought about by other conditions. If we continue to look in this way, we'll see that nothing has been left out; everything in the cosmos has come together to bring us this table. Looking deeply at the sunshine, the leaves of the tree, and the clouds, we can see the table. The one can be seen in the all, and the all can be seen in the one. One cause is never enough to bring about an effect. A cause must, at the same time, be an effect, and every effect must also be the cause of something else. Cause and effect inter-are; they give rise to each other. The idea of a first or a single cause, something that does not itself need a cause, cannot be applied.

Our difficulties arise when we forget this teaching and become attached to ideas and to things, believing that they are independent and permanent. When we embrace the interdependent nature of all things, forsaking all extremes, we will be on the path of a more peaceful and joy-filled existence.

The Sutra on the Middle Way

I heard these words of the Buddha one time when the Lord was staying at the guesthouse in a forest of the district of Nala. At that time, the Venerable Kaccayana came to visit him and asked, "The Tathagata has spoken of Right View. How would the Tathagata describe Right View?"

The Buddha told the venerable monk, "People in the world tend to believe in one of two views: the view of being or the view of nonbeing. That is because they are bound to wrong perception. It is wrong perception that leads to the concepts of being and nonbeing. Kaccayana, most people are bound to the internal formations of discrimination and preference, grasping and attachment. Those who are not bound to the internal knots of grasping and attachment no longer imagine and cling to the idea of a self. They understand, for example, that suffering comes to be when conditions are favorable, and that it fades away when conditions are no longer favorable. They no longer have any doubts. Their understanding has not come to them through others; it is their own insight. This insight is called Right View, and this is the way the Tathagata would describe Right View.

"How is this so? When a person who has correct insight observes the coming to be of the world, the idea of nonbeing does not arise in her, and when she observes the fading away of the world, the idea of being does not arise in her mind. Kaccayana, viewing the world as being is an extreme; viewing it as nonbeing is another extreme. The Tathagata avoids these two extremes and teaches the Dharma dwelling in the Middle Way.

"The Middle Way says that this is, because that is; this is not, because that is not. Because there is ignorance, there are impulses; because there are impulses, there is consciousness; because there is consciousness, there is the psyche-soma; because there is the psyche-soma, there are the six senses; because there are the six senses, there is contact; because there is contact, there is feeling; because there is feeling, there is craving; because there is craving, there is grasping; because there is grasping, there is becoming; because there is becoming, there is birth; because there is birth, there are old age, death, grief, and sorrow. That is how this entire mass of suffering arises. But with the fading away of ignorance, impulses cease; with the fading away of impulses, consciousness ceases; ...and finally birth, old age, death, grief, and sorrow will fade away. That is how this entire mass of suffering ceases."

After listening to the Buddha, the Venerable Kaccayana was enlightened and liberated from sorrow. He was able to untie all of his internal knots and attain arhatship.

Samyukta Agama 301

Commentary on the Sutra

Right View

In this sutra we study Right View in the light of the Middle Way. The Middle way means not being caught in pairs of opposites like "exists" or "does not exist." The Middle Way could be wrongly interpreted as meaning that "exists" and "does not exist" are both possible, and that the Middle Way goes between them. But in fact it means that "exists" and "does not exist" are both ideas we need to go beyond. Our insight of Right View is based on our observation of conditioned existence.

> I heard these words of the Buddha one time when the Lord was staying at the guest-house in a forest of the district of Nala.

The Chinese version of the sutra says Buddha delivered this discourse in Nala, in the kingdom of Magadha. The Pali version says it was delivered in Savatthi (*Shravasti*), in the kingdom of Koshala. Magadha and Koshala are ancient kingdoms of the Ganges River basin.

> At that time, the Venerable Kaccayana came to visit him and asked, "The Tathagata has spoken of Right View. How would the Tathagata describe Right View?"

The Venerable Kaccayana was a high monk in the Buddha's Sangha. His question is about Right View, and the Buddha responds by speaking of the Middle Way. The Middle Way avoids extreme views and dualistic thinking. Because we have wrong views, we have wrong perceptions. Wrong perceptions are the ground of all afflictions: fear, anger, discrimination, despair. All these kinds of afflictions are born from wrong perceptions. Looking deeply into the wrong perceptions, ideas, and notions that are at the base of our suffering is the most important practice in Buddhist meditation.

Our happiness and the happiness of those around us depend on our degree of Right View. But Right View is not an ideology, a system, or even a path. It cannot be described; we can only point in the correct direction. Even a teacher cannot transmit Right View. A teacher can help us identify the seed of Right View that is already there in our garden, and help us gain confidence, and show us how to practice, to entrust that seed to the soil of our daily life.

Store consciousness is the place where all our

experiences can be found. It is like the hard disk in a computer. Everything we've heard and seen, every experience of our life has been stored there. Mind consciousness—our conscious mind—plays the role of the gardener. We cultivate the soil with our daily practice of mindfulness, helping the seed of Right View to manifest and grow.

So mind consciousness is the gardener, cultivating the soil and nourishing the seed of Right View with our daily practice of mindfulness. Buddhist meditation is an attempt to integrate mind consciousness in every moment of our daily life so we are aware of what is going on within us and around us, so that we can truly be ourselves. Otherwise we're on automatic pilot and we're not really living our life.

The Middle Way is not caught in pairs of opposites, such as being and nonbeing; coming and going; birth and death; same and different; exists and does not exist. These are ideas we need to go beyond. Shakespeare said, "To be, or not to be: that is the question." But in Buddhism, we go beyond the idea of being and not being. Because we have wrong views, we have wrong perceptions, and because of those wrong perceptions we think that this world is real, or that this world is not real.

The phrase "wrong view" itself is not exactly accurate. Relatively speaking, there are right views and there are wrong views. But if we look more deeply, we see that *all views are wrong views*. No view can ever be the truth. It is just the view from one point; that is why it is called a "point of view." If we go to another point, we will see things differently and realize that our first view was not entirely right. Buddhism is not a collection of views. It is a practice that helps us eliminate wrong views. The quality of our views can always be improved. From the viewpoint of the ultimate reality, Right View is the absence of all views.

At the base of our views are our perceptions (*samjña*). In the Chinese character for perception, the upper part of the character means "mark," "sign," or "appearance," and the lower part means "mind" or "spirit." A perception always has a "mark," and in many cases that mark is illusory. The Buddha advised us not to be fooled by what we perceive.

In the Diamond Sutra, the Buddha told the monk Subhuti, "In a place where there is something that can be distinguished by signs, in that place there is deception."* The Buddha taught on many occasions that most of our perceptions are erroneous, and that most of our suffering comes from wrong perceptions. We have to ask ourselves again and again, "Am

* See Thich Nhat Hanh, *The Diamond that Cuts through Illusion* (Berkeley, CA: Parallax, Press, 1992).

I sure?" Until we see clearly, our wrong perceptions will prevent us from having Right View.

To perceive always means to perceive *something*. We believe that the object of our perception is separate from the subject, but that is not correct. When we perceive a mountain, the mountain is the object of our perception. When we perceive the moon, the moon is the object of our perception. When we say, "I can see my consciousness in the flower," it means we can see the cloud, the sunshine, the earth, and the minerals in it. But how can we see our consciousness in a flower? The flower *is* our consciousness. Perception means the coming into existence of the perceiver and the perceived. The flower that we are looking at is part of our consciousness. The idea that our consciousness is outside of the flower is deluded. It is impossible to have a subject without an object. It is impossible to remove one and retain the other.

> The Buddha told the venerable monk, "People in the world tend to believe in one of two views: the view of being or the view of nonbeing. That is because they are bound to wrong perception. It is wrong perception that leads to the concepts of being and nonbeing."

These words of the sutra are very clear. We have wrong views, we have wrong perceptions, and because of those wrong perceptions we think that this world is real, or that this world is not real. We have to throw away these wrong perceptions. Throwing away is stronger than "letting go." It takes insight and courage to throw away an idea. If we've suffered, it may be because we've entertained an idea that we haven't been able to release.

There are those of us who believe in an immortal soul, that after the disintegration of this body, the immortal soul continues to live on and doesn't change. We know that everything is changing, that everything is impermanent. So the notion that there is an immortal soul that remains itself forever and ever is a wrong view called permanence. The other extreme is annihilation: the idea that something can disappear forever and that after we die, nothing is left. That is also a wrong view. We are used to seeing the world as a series of opposites.

When we invite a flame to manifest, we can ask the flame, "Dear little flame, where have you come from?" We have the notion of coming and going. But the flame has not come from anywhere. Her nature is the nature of no coming. When conditions come together, she manifests. So coming is a notion. Going is another notion. When the flame is extinguished we can ask, "Dear little flame, where have you gone?" And the flame will answer, "I have gone nowhere. When conditions are no longer sufficient, I cease my manifestation. My nature is no coming, no going." Even when the flame is manifesting, the flame of one second is not the flame of the next. There is input and output, birth and death, at every moment.

Several years ago during a retreat in northern Germany, the Sangha married a couple. The next morning the couple came before the Sangha of mindfulness to report to us on the teaching of impermanence and neither the same nor different. The young man looked at his bride and asked this question: "Darling, are you the same person I married yesterday or are you a different one?" Because things are impermanent, nothing can remain the same in two consecutive days or moments. When you love, you worry a little bit that the other person may no longer love you. You want to be assured all the time that she still loves you. The young woman looked at her new husband, smiling, and said: "Don't worry, my dear, although I am not exactly the same person you married yesterday, I am not a different person either." That is the truth. The notions of sameness and otherness should be thrown away. If we are successful in our contemplation of impermanence, permanence no longer makes sense.

> "Kaccayana, most people are bound to the internal formations of discrimination and preference, grasping and attachment. Those who are not bound to the internal knots of grasping and attachment no longer imagine and cling to the idea of a self."

Here we have two words: "grasping," which means not letting go; and "attachment," which is like a crab catching hold of us and not letting us go. What catches us and will not let us go are our ideas, our wrong perceptions. We're caught in our ideas and perceptions, and therefore we're attached to them.

We each have a view of the universe. That view may be called relativity or uncertainty or probability or string theory; there are many kinds of views. It's okay to propose views, but if you want to make progress on the path of inquiry, you should be able to be ready to throw away your view. It's like climbing a ladder, coming to the fifth rung, and thinking you're on the highest rung. That idea prevents you from climbing to the sixth, and the seventh rung. You are caught. So in order to come to the sixth and the seventh, you have to release the fifth. That is the process of learning proposed by the Buddha. Buddhism fully practiced is free from dogmatism. If you worship something as a dogma, as absolute truth, you are not a good practitioner. You must be totally free, even from the teachings of the Buddha. The teachings of the Buddha are offered as instruments, not as absolute truth.

We have the habit of distinguishing between wrong views and right views. We say that permanence is a wrong view, and we use the Right View of impermanence to overcome the view of permanence. But you also have to be free from the view of impermanence.

The truly Right View, as the sutra tells us, is the absence of all views. According to the teachings of the Buddha, we have to throw away all views, including the so-called right views. Reality, things as they are, cannot be described in terms of notions and views. That is why so-called "right views" are only instruments to help us.

In the Ratnakuta Sutra, the Accumulation of Jewels, the Buddha said that if you are attached to the notion of existence, then the notion of emptiness might help to rescue you. But if you are caught by the notion of emptiness, no one can rescue you. You have to see the Dharma like that also. You should be free from the true teachings, let alone from the teachings that are not true. In the Diamond Sutra the Buddha says: "All teachings must be abandoned, not to mention non-teachings." The practice of throwing away your notions and views is so important. Liberation will not be possible without this practice of throwing away.

> "Those who are not bound to the internal knots of grasping and attachment no longer imagine and cling to the idea of a self."

The word "imagine" is the translation of the Chinese word that means to measure, to estimate, to conceive of. We have a conception about something. We say it's important or it's not important. We say it exists or it doesn't exist. Wrong perception means that we imagine things about the truth. We load this idea and that idea on to the truth. Actually the truth is not like that, but we think it's like that. Although we know that nothing is permanent, in our everyday life we think of things as permanent. Even if we understand the idea that a separate "self" is a misperception, most of our thinking is based on seeing things as having a self. This kind of thinking is dangerous. These ideas tend to make us feel secure. But in fact they're based on wrong perception. The basis for all our grasping and imagining is our ideas.

At the center of our grasping and imagining,

at the center of all our wrong perceptions is our idea about self. We think there's something called a "self," that there is a "me" and "mine." We have the idea that "I" exist, and that there are things that belong to "me," that are "mine." But who is this self?

When we look at a flower and ask, "Who is opening?" we don't need an "I" which is born, which grows old, and which will die. We think that if there's birth, there has to be an "I" that is born, if there is aging, there has to be an "I" that grows old, and if there is death, there has to be someone who will die.

In truth, birth is simply birth, old age is simply old age, death is death; there is no "I" in that. It is only when we are caught in the idea of self that we say there has to be an "I." Does the flower have a soul, a self, within it? Does it need a self in order to be born, to open, and to fade; does it need an "I" in order to exist? For there to be rain, there doesn't have to be an "I." Rain happens; you don't have to ask, "Who is falling?" In many languages, we have to say "it" is raining, implying there is a self that is raining. But if there is rain, is there a self in the rain? We get used to this way of speaking, that there has to be a subject, a self, and only then can there be an action. In English we say, "It rains." In Vietnamese we say, "The sky is raining" or "the weather is raining."

When we say, "I know the wind is blowing,"

we can divide this sentence into two phrases. One is "I know," the other, "the wind is blowing." This is truly a strange statement. How can there be wind that doesn't blow? As soon as you have wind, you have blowing; without blowing there is no wind, the blowing is part of the wind. Why not just say, "the wind"? It's the same when we say, "A cloud is floating in the sky" or "a flower is opening." If a cloud is not floating in the sky, then it's still the water in the river; if a flower is not open, it's not yet a flower, but a bud. There is also the phrase, "I know." Do we have to have an "I"? Just to say "know" would be enough, we don't need "I." "Know" is a verb, so it requires a subject, and therefore we have to have the word "I." If we wish to say the truth, just to say "rain" or "wind" or "cloud" is enough.

We've become accustomed to the habit of thinking and speaking in terms of a subject, a self. This has been happening for so many past generations. But, unfortunately, this idea that there must be a subject hides the truth from us.

Dependent Co-arising

> "They understand, for example, that suffering comes to be when conditions are favorable, and that it fades away when conditions are no longer favorable. They no longer have any doubts."

Here the Buddha talks about suffering simply as a phenomenon, just like a picture or a table. The inclusion of the words "for example" makes this clear. Suffering is just being used as an example to represent all phenomena.

The Buddha is talking about causes and conditions. We find out about the Middle Way by observing and learning about conditioned existence. Cause and effect co-arise and everything is a result of multiple causes and conditions. The egg is in the chicken and the chicken is in the egg. Chicken and egg arise in mutual dependence. Nothing can arise independently.

"Causes and conditions," and "Dependent Co-arising" carry a similar meaning and are at the heart of the Buddha's teaching. "Causes" refers to the seed or principle condition. "Conditions" refers to the other necessary conditions that are not the principal ones. In the Chinese character for "cause," the word "great" is pictured inside four walls. If something is to become great, it must break through those boundaries. When you look at a mustard seed, it's small; the conditions aren't there for it to be large. But when the mustard seed is put into the earth and watered, it becomes a great plant. The conditions to bring the mustard seed to fruition are water, earth, fertilizer, warmth, and so on. Notice that the conditions are also causes. But the primary cause, of course, is the seed itself. The subsidiary causes are the conditions necessary to support the primary cause to develop.

In talking about causes and conditions, the Buddha used the term "Dependent Co-arising" (*pratitya samutpada*). "Dependent" means relying on each other. "Co" means together, simultaneously. Nothing can arise alone or stand on its own; everything is dependent upon everything else.

In the United States, although we celebrate Independence Day, we cannot really live without being dependent on other countries. Maybe we should celebrate "Interdependence Day," since one country has to depend on other countries in order to exist.

When we have a feeling of suffering and we look deeply into it, we can see that the suffering comes from various conditions that have caused it to arise. When we look deeply at a flower, we see that many conditions have come together to make the flower possible.

The same is true of a cloud or a table; when the conditions necessary for them to be are not there, then they will not be there. A person who observes in this way sees clearly and no longer has any doubts. We see that everything comes to be because of the coming together of favorable conditions, and when those conditions fall apart, that thing can no longer exist.

> "Their understanding has not come to them through others; it is their own insight." This insight is called Right View, and this is the way the Tathagata would describe Right View.*

Everything comes to be because of various causes and conditions. Don't believe this just because the

---

* The Buddha uses the term "Tathagata" when speaking of himself.

Buddha said it. Believe it because you've looked deeply and seen it for yourself. The Buddha always asks that we experience these things for ourselves and not accept them based on the words, teachings, or ideas of anyone else, including the Buddha. We don't want to repeat, like a parrot, the things that other people have said.

We have suffering; everyone has suffering. When we look deeply into the heart of that suffering, we see the causes and conditions near and far which have brought it about. We can see this on our own. No one else has to say this to us. It's with our own wisdom that we look into our suffering. Because we've been able to see this for ourselves, we have no doubts about our insight, we know that it is so. That insight comes from us, it's not something we receive from someone else.

Regardless of the number, when conditions that are related to each other come together, they bring about a phenomenon, and we have a perception of that phenomenon. Whether a Buddha is or is not present in the world to teach about it, Dependent Co-arising remains the basis of everything. This truth, or law, is always there in the field of all phenomena. This truth is always present in all dharma realms.

"How is this so? When a person who has correct insight observes the coming to be of the world, the idea of nonbeing does not arise in her, and when she observes the fading away of the world, the idea of being does not arise in her mind."

"Being" or "becoming" occur in the *lokadhatu*. The lokadhatu refers to this world, the world of suffering, where things appear to be born and to die and to exist independently of each other; the grapefruit is independent of the lemon. But in the *dharmadhatu*, the realm of "things as they are," the lotus is not different from the meditation hall, a man is not different from his brother, all things are interconnected; in the one is the all and the all is in the one. All dharmas, all phenomena, dwell in the dharmadhatu. If we can touch them deeply, we can be in touch with their no-birth and no-death nature. This is the world of the dharmadhatu, nirvana. It is our way of living that determines whether we're living in the dharmadhatu or in the lokadhatu.

According to the teachings on Dependent Co-arising, all phenomena dwell in their Dharma nature, their nature of no-birth and no-death. We have our Dharma nature; the flower has its Dharma nature. If we can be in touch with that nature, we go beyond ideas of being born and dying. If we can be in touch with the Dharma nature of the flower, we won't see the flower as something that blooms and then dies, and that is separate from other things.

It is clear that the world is in the process of manifesting. It is clear that the flower is manifesting. So we cannot say it doesn't exist. We see that suffering is manifesting; we can't say that suffering isn't there. But when we can see and know something as it really is, we won't attach to it, and we won't weigh it down and burden it with ideas.

> "When a person who has correct insight observes the coming to be of the world, the idea of nonbeing does not arise in her, and when she observes the fading away of the world, the idea of being does not arise in her mind. Kaccayana, viewing the world as being is an extreme; viewing it as nonbeing is another extreme. The Tathagata avoids these two extremes and teaches the Dharma dwelling in the Middle Way."

The notions that life span is this body or is not this body are two of the "extreme views" spoken of in the Sutra. The Middle Way goes beyond ideas of being and nonbeing, birth and death, one and many, coming and going, same and different.

The notions of existing and not existing come from our wrong perceptions. The Buddha says that we should go beyond the ideas of "exists" and "does not exist." When something manifests, we have the tendency to say it exists; and when it no longer manifests, to say it doesn't exist. This is a mistake that many of us make.

Plum Village, where I live, is situated amidst fields of sunflowers. When we do walking meditation in April, we don't see any sunflowers so we say, "There are no sunflowers," and we think of them as not existing. But a farmer driving along the road in April will see things differently. If we were to say to the farmer, "There are no sunflowers," he may say, "Yes, there are," because he has planted the seed. Then in May or June sunflowers will appear.

We're very quick to come to the conclusion that something doesn't exist. The farmer knows very well that in two months' time the field will be full of sunflowers. But we who don't know anything about farming will say, "There are no sunflowers," but our view is not in accord with reality.

The teachings of the Buddha are always the Middle Way, the way that goes beyond ideas of being and nonbeing, birth and death, one and many, coming and going, same and different, as well as ideas of not being born, not dying, not one, not many, and so on. The Tathagata avoids these extremes.

In eleventh century Vietnam, a monk asked his meditation master, "Where is the place beyond birth and death?" The master replied, "In the midst of birth and death." If you abandon birth and death in order to find nirvana, you will not find nirvana; nirvana is in birth and death. Looking deeply into the phenomenological world, we touch the true nature, the noumenal world.

> "The Middle Way says that this is, because that is; this is not, because that is not."

These words are so simple but they're very deep. "This is, because that is." This is the meaning of interdependence. "This arises because that arises." The word "arises" is better than the word "born." This is the definition of Dependent Co-arising and it is repeated many times in the Original Buddhist sutras. "This is, therefore that is." "This is, because that is; this is not, because that is not." "This ceases to be, because that ceases to be." "This is like this, because that is like that." That is the best definition of Dependent Co-arising that we can give. If we smile, the mirror smiles back at us. If we are kind to others, they will be kind to us.

When people ask such questions as: "Is there a

teaching in Buddhism about how the world came to exist?" "Who created the world?" "When did it begin and when will it end?" there is only one thing we can do, and that is to cite this phrase: "This is because that is; this is not because that is not." This is born because that is born. This ends because that ends. The flower is because the sunlight is because the seed is because the Earth is. This thing can be because other things are there. This is the teaching of Dependent Co-arising, and it is presented so simply. "This is because that is" is the highest reply we can give to questions about the existence of the world.

Just like all other things, time is a conditioned phenomenon. Time is conditioned by space, by earth, by water, by everything in the cosmos. This is true for a flower, it is true for our suffering, and it is true for all phenomena in the world. The question "What is the first cause?" comes from our ignorance. Questions such as: "Who created the world?" "Is there such a thing as time or not?" "When did time begin?" become very naive when we understand the teachings on the Middle Way. When we've understood these teachings we can go deeply into the teachings of Dependent Co-arising. Time is there because of space, space is there because of time; they are dependent on each other. This manifests because that manifests. This is latent because that is latent. We don't have to go to a teacher or a religion to answer these things. We only have to look deeply to be able to see for ourselves.

This is because that is. This arises because that arises. For there to be a father, there has to be a child; and if there is a child, there has to be a father. If there's an elder brother, there must be a younger brother; and if there's a younger brother it's because there is an elder brother. There is night because there is day. These things rely on each other in order to exist.

> "Because there is ignorance, there are impulses; because there are impulses, there is consciousness; because there is consciousness, there is the psyche-soma; because there is the psyche-soma, there are the six senses; because there are the six senses, there is contact; because there is contact, there is feeling; because there is feeling, there is craving; because there is craving, there is grasping; because there is grasping, there is becoming; because there is becoming, there is birth; because there is birth, there are old age, death, grief, and sorrow. That is how this entire mass of suffering

arises. But with the fading away of ignorance, impulses cease; with the fading away of impulses, consciousness ceases; . . . and finally birth, old age, grief, death, and sorrow will fade away. That is how this entire mass of suffering ceases."

After listening to the Buddha, the Venerable Kaccayana was enlightened and liberated from sorrow. He was able to untie all of his internal knots and attain arhatship.

Here the Buddha speaks about the twelve links of Dependent Co-arising. The first link is ignorance (*avidya*), and it informs all the other links. Vidya means seeing, understanding, or light. Avidya means blindness, lack of understanding, or lack of light. The second link is volitional action (*samskara*), motivating energy, and the impulse to cling to being. The third link is consciousness (*vijñana*). Consciousness is filled with unwholesome and erroneous tendencies, which bring about suffering. The fourth link is the psyche-soma, mind and body. It is also called *namarupa*, name and form, referring to the mental element and physical element of our being. Both mind and body are objects of our consciousness. The fifth link is the six *ayatanas*, which are the six sense organs (eyes, ears, nose, tongue, body, and mind) accompanied by their objects (forms, sounds, smells, tastes, tactile objects, and objects of mind). These six ayatanas do not exist separately from mind/body (the fourth link), but are listed separately to help us see them more clearly.

The sixth link is the contact (*sparsha*) between sense organ and sense object; this brings about sense consciousness. When eyes and form, ears and sound, nose and smell, tongue and taste, body and touch, and mind and object of mind come into contact, sense consciousness is born. Contact is an important basis for feelings (*vedana*), the seventh link. Feelings can be pleasant, unpleasant, neutral, or mixed. We tend to become very attached to our feelings. The eighth link is craving (*trishna*), or desire. The ninth link is grasping, or attachment (*upadana*). It means we are caught, in thrall to the object. The tenth link is becoming (*bhava*), being, or coming to be. Because we desire something, it comes to be. We have to look deeply to know what we really want. The eleventh link is birth (*jati*). The twelfth link is old age, death, and decay (*jaramarana*).

The Buddha said that the teachings on the twelve links of causation are the essence of his teaching. The twelve links were never meant to be understood in a linear way, with each link leading only to the next. Each link could not exist without all the others; in this way we can say the links are "empty." Each link in the chain of Dependent Co-arising is both a cause and an effect of all the other links in the chain. In each there is ignorance, in each there is consciousness.

Studying the twelve links of Dependent Co-arising helps us diminish the element of ignorance and increase the element of clarity. When our ignorance is diminished, craving, hatred, pride, doubt, and views are also diminished, and love, compassion, joy, and equanimity are increased.

If you look into your body or your emotion in one moment of your daily life, you will see that all of the twelve links are present in that moment. These twelve causes and conditions lean on each other, are committed to each other, and bring about the great mass of suffering. Each one of the twelve links is in relationship with the other eleven. If you don't practice mindfully, you allow this cycle of suffering to continue.

When we practice mindfulness, we can see that the twelve links of Dependent Co-arising can be informed by wisdom instead of by ignorance. When wisdom is the first link, all the other links are influenced by it. For example, sometimes a feeling is accompanied not by ignorance, but by understanding, lucidity, or loving kindness, which can result in compassionate action. To say that feeling brings about craving is not precise enough. Feeling with attachment and ignorance brings about craving. In the cycle based on ignorance, living beings drift and sink because of their deluded minds. When feelings are conditioned by wisdom, Dependent Co-arising can also bring about mindfulness, liberation, and nirvana. The cycle based on clarity and awareness is the one in which the bodhisattvas realize awakening.

When you light up the lamp of awareness, you will see how the twelve links of Dependent Co-arising are working. You will say, "Let's not let the links work like that anymore, we've suffered enough already." When we bring mindfulness into the picture, our ignorance becomes less dark, and clarity arises. From mindfulness arises the clarity of consciousness. Within consciousness there is ignorance, but there is also the seed of awakening and mindfulness. If we light up the lamp of mindfulness it will make the darkness disappear.

Very often our suffering and despair help us to awaken; thus, clarity can come from ignorance. When the lamp is alight the ignorance in our attachment and despair will weaken and transform. Our clarity gives rise to *bodhicitta*, the great aspiration. If you have a great aspiration, it's because you've seen suffering, have awakened to the presence of suffering, and want to put an end to it. Clarity brings about bodhicitta, the aspiration to attain enlightenment for the benefit of all living beings. The great aspiration gives us the insight that we have to be there for all suffering beings.

In the cycle based on wisdom, we have something that's equivalent to psyche-soma. That is the *nirmanakaya*, the transformation body of the Buddha. We see our connection with all other living beings. Living beings contain hatred and darkness. Now our presence, like that of the flower, can bring freshness and happiness. The nirmanakaya is the form in which a bodhisattva is present. There are still the six senses, but now wisdom is their basis. For an ordinary person, the six senses are the cause of bondage because they have ignorance at their base. In the transformation body of the bodhisattva, the six senses are there, but they do not have ignorance in them; they have the great vow in them.

The transformation body of the bodhisattva is also in contact with the sense objects. There has to be contact between the sense organs and the object because the bodhisattva is in the world in order to be in touch. In that contact there is mindfulness. With mindfulness, there is clarity, great aspiration, and wisdom. Contact leads to feeling, but now feeling contains mindfulness.

When there is mindfulness, there will still be pleasant, unpleasant, and neutral feelings. But these feelings no longer contain ignorance; instead they contain great aspiration and wisdom. When there is a painful feeling the bodhisattva knows it is a painful feeling. When there is a pleasant feeling the bodhisattva knows it is a pleasant feeling. So there is no wrong perception within feelings; they are recognized for what they are. A bodhisattva can share the suffering of living beings. When she sees someone in great pain, she feels compassion, she suffers. But that kind of suffering increases her wisdom and nourishes her great aspiration. When there is mindfulness of feelings, they don't lead to craving, but to compassion and loving kindness. Seeing living beings suffer, the bodhisattva gives rise, not to anger, but to love and the mind of compassion. Living beings suffer, and because they suffer, they crave and are attached, and they spread their suffering around them. But the bodhisattva, although she feels this suffering, is still free, and has compassion and loving kindness. Loving kindness and compassion contain clarity; they are elements of true love; they don't lead to attachment, but to freedom. It's because the bodhisattva has compassion and love that she is always able to maintain her freedom. If clarity and great aspiration are lost, freedom is lost at the same time.

The substance of a bodhisattva is freedom. When the bodhisattva goes into life, she's not motivated by attachment or bondage, but by the great aspiration. The bodhisattva dwells in the dharmadhatu but is motivated by compassion and loving kindness to go into the world of birth and death. While he dwells in freedom in the dharmadhatu, he doesn't abandon the beings who are drifting and sinking in the world of suffering.

Dependent Co-arising is sometimes called great emptiness (*mahasunyata*). The word "emptiness" means free from all notions, ideas, and attachments. You can't say phenomena don't exist, you can't say they do exist, you can't say they're born or they die, you can't say phenomena are the same, you can't say they're different; all phenomena lie in their nature of emptiness and cannot be grasped.

This poem from Nagarjuna talks about emptiness and Dependent Co-arising:

All phenomena that arise interdependently,
I say that they are empty.
Words come to an end, because their message is false.
Words come to an end, because there is a Middle Way.

If we look carefully into the twelve links of Dependent Co-arising, we will see the teachings of emptiness. The Buddha said, whoever sees Dependent Co-arising sees the Buddha, and whoever has seen the Buddha has seen Dependent Co-arising. In our daily lives, we may ask, "Who am I? What am I doing here? Where did I come from? Where will I go?" These are philosophical questions. The Buddha said the reason we ask such questions is that we are caught in the idea of self, in the idea of me and mine. If we can see Dependent Co-arising, we will not ask these questions anymore.

The Buddha advises us not to study philosophy, but to give our time to looking deeply into reality, and to being able to see the true abiding of all dharmas, the suchness of all dharmas, the emptiness of all dharmas. When we see this, we will no longer be caught in the idea of "self," the idea of "is" and "is not," and in asking philosophical questions. When we see the nature of Dependent Co-arising, worldly views and worldly knowledge will no longer catch us, and we will go beyond the internal formations that are based on them.

When we can meditate on Dependent Co-arising we go beyond all these questions. The Buddha said, when we go beyond these ideas, we're like a palm tree that has had its top cut off. All our wrong perceptions will no longer arise. When we've been able to see the nature of interdependent arising, we'll overcome ideas of self, living being, and so on, and ignorance and suffering will no longer touch us. We'll no longer suffer because of our wrong views.

Walking the Path of the Middle Way

One day Buddha asked the monk Sona:

"Is it true that before you became a monk you were a musician?"
Sona replied that it was so.
The Buddha asked, "What happens if the string of your instrument is too loose?"
"When you pluck it, there will be no sound," Sona replied.
"What happens when the string is too taut?"
"It will break."
"The practice of the Way is the same," the Buddha said.

The Sutra on the Middle Way has profound and wonderful meaning. But only when we discover how to apply the teachings in it to our daily lives can they be truly beneficial. Even when we are able to talk eloquently about the Middle Way, no-self, or Dependent Co-arising, we still need to ask: How can these teachings be put into practice every day?

The first way is to notice our attachment to the teachings themselves. Not only do views such as permanence and self need to be transcended, so do impermanence, nonself, and nirvana. The Buddha says the teachings are like a raft that helps us to the other shore. Once there, we leave the raft on the shore for others to use. The teachings, like the raft, need to be released. It's said that near the end of his life the Buddha said, "In forty-five years of teaching I have not said anything." In fact he said a lot things, but he didn't want his listeners to get caught in his words.

For ease of understanding, we speak of teachings such as impermanence, nonself, and interbeing as right views. But we know these are teachings to help us, they're not theories. For example, the notion of impermanence is to help us overcome the notion of permanence; it's not a truth to be worshipped. The teachings need to be handled skillfully so we don't get caught in them.

When presenting the twelve links of Dependent Co-arising, the Buddha says that "ignorance gives rise to impulses." "Ignorance" means that we don't understand what is happening, so we behave in a certain way. If we were able to see clearly, we would behave differently. Each one of us is caught, to a larger or a smaller extent, in our emotions, in our difficulties, and in our experiences of suffering in the past. Because we're caught, we repeat the same suffering over and over again. We have a habit energy of reacting to circumstances in a rote way. We tell ourselves that the next time that happens we won't react like this, we'll react differently. We're very determined; we make a promise to ourselves. But when that thing happens again, we still react in the old way—as we did 200 years ago. So why do we keep repeating this? Every time we behave like this we make others suffer and we make ourselves suffer.

Our habit energy is what causes us to repeat the same behavior thousands of times. Habit energy pushes us to run, to always be doing something, to be lost in thoughts of the past or the future and to blame others for our suffering. And that energy does not allow us to be peaceful and happy in the present moment.

The practice of mindfulness helps us to recognize that habitual energy. Every time we can recognize the habit energy in us, we are able to stop and to enjoy the present moment. The energy of mindfulness is the best energy to help us embrace our habit energy and transform it.

The energy of mindfulness is the full awareness of the present moment. This energy is generated from the practice of mindful breathing, mindful walking, mindful drinking, mindful eating, and so on. The energy of mindfulness carries within itself the energy of concentration. When you are mindful of something, whether that something is a flower, a friend, or a cup of tea, you become concentrated on the object of your mindfulness. The more you are mindful, the more concentrated you become. The energy of concentration is born from the energy of mindfulness. And if you are concentrated enough, the energy of concentration contains the energy of insight. Mindfulness, concentration, and insight are the energies that make up the Buddha. These three kinds of energy can transform habit energy and lead to healing and nourishment.

A few days of practicing mindful breathing and mindful walking can make a big difference. And the practice should be pleasant, should not be hard labor. When you breathe in, you bring attention to your in-breath. "Breathing in, I know I am breathing in; breathing in, I feel alive." In that breath is your happiness.

Whenever habit energies arise, we can accept and recognize them and then they won't push us to behave in negative ways. We can say to our habit energy, "I will look after you, habit energy, I will discover what your root is."

Often, when I'm talking to a large group, giving

a Dharma talk, I'll tell a story. Suppose I tell the story of a monk who doesn't practice, who just goes from festival to festival, memorial service to memorial service in different temples. He doesn't organize ceremonies in his own temple, but when he sees other temples celebrating, he goes to them. And he stays there all day. I may be telling this story just for fun, but some people may feel I'm reprimanding them specifically. I have no intention of directing what I'm saying to those particular people, but because they have that habit energy, they receive the story like an arrow, wounding them. When we suffer we make those around us suffer. We think we are the only person who is suffering, but in fact we are creating suffering for other people.

After a retreat I held, one of the students wrote to me and said: "I'd never felt so happy and secure as in this retreat, because nobody was allowed to talk. So I knew nobody would come and say things which would hurt me or say unkind things to me or about me." When I read that, I thought this person must have suffered a lot in the past. Probably people in his family had said things to him that hurt him very badly. I felt compassion for him. I knew how much he must have suffered. So we have to look back at our suffering and see how, without the energy of mindfulness, we suffer and we make others suffer.

We may feel that it is because of someone's clumsiness or lack of mindfulness that we suffer, but we often do the same to others. Only when our light of mindfulness shines on all of us will we be able to take steps in lightness, ease, and freedom.

The suffering that we have borne in the past is immeasurable. Compared with our suffering of the past, our suffering of today is very small. So why do we continue to make each other suffer? In the great ocean the big fish are eating the little fish. A baby fish is swimming along and suddenly a huge fish comes up behind, opens up its mouth, and the little fish becomes the food of the big fish. There are bears that go down to the river when they are hungry and catch the fish in their paws and eat them. "Why aren't the other fish caught and eaten? Why am I caught and eaten today?" Ducklings are following their mother, and while the mother duck is eating worms, a large bird snatches up one of the baby ducklings. This is the kind of suffering we have been through in the past. We are that duckling; we are that fish. Sometimes the mother hen sees the danger and puts out her wings to protect her baby chicks, so that the large bird doesn't swoop down and take them away. Sometimes we've wanted to protect our children, but we haven't succeeded. And these sufferings take place in life all the time. We have suffered so much as birds, as fish, as trees, and all those sufferings have become a great mass of suffering within us.

Our Sangha, our practice community, plays an important role in helping us put an end to the habit energy of suffering. The Sutra on the Middle Way reminds us that the idea of a self is just a shell. Only when we can get out of the stiff shell of the self can we see that our suffering in the present is the suffering of our ancestors and of our descendants. We are the continuation of our mother; we are our mother. Our children, our students are already in us, suffering with us. So we should not waste a moment or a day of our practice.

Every day is an opportunity for us to practice liberation—liberating our ancestors and our descendants within us. With meditation, we can relive the moments of our life that have been full of fear and suffering, and we can practice mindful breathing and breathe for all our ancestors and all our descendants. When I am breathing, I'm not breathing for one mother and one child, but for many mothers and many children. Breathing like that for ten minutes can bring liberation if we practice properly, and the insight we use in our practice is the insight of the Middle Way.

The teachings on Right View and Dependent Co-arising also offer us guidance on how to be with others. When we look deeply into others, we are looking deeply into ourselves at the same time. If we think the other person is someone other than us, that his or her success or failure has nothing to do with us, then we have not been successful in our looking deeply. The happiness of that person is linked to our own happiness. If we're not happy, the other person can't be happy, and our larger community will not be happy.

The monkey knows that the fruit with a lot of prickles is very sweet inside, so he uses a stone to break the skin of that prickly fruit. There may be people in our life we feel are too difficult to talk to or be with. We see them as severe, not generous, not able to embrace and accept us. But that is only our first experience. There may be a great deal of love and compassion in that person, which is obscured by habit energies. If we look deeply and see what is obstructing that person, we can help them. If we can break the shell of habit energies we will enjoy the sweetness of the love that is inside. We can be like the monkey who is able to pierce the tough prickly skin and savor the fruit inside.

The aim of Buddhist practice is to go from the field of phenomena down into the level of substance, of true nature. We go from being caught in conventional designations—parent, child, I, you, flower, cloud, coming, going—down into the level of the Middle Way which goes beyond all conventional designation. Anger and hatred arise because we are caught in the conventional designation. If we look deeply and carefully, we will see ourselves in our parents and will see our parents in ourselves. When we can see that, we can be in touch with a very deep level of reality, and our suffering and sadness will evaporate.

If we continue to be imprisoned by the habit energies of the past, we will never liberate ourselves, nor can we liberate the thousands of generations of ancestors and descendants in us. But if in our daily lives, while we are washing up, cleaning the vegetables, driving the car, working in the garden, or watering the plants, we use that time to truly look at ourselves and each other to see our true nature and the true nature of others, we can gradually get out of the ropes that bind us. Our fear, our sorrow, our complexes are all born from our discriminating ideas of coming and going, self and the other. Looking deeply in our daily life like this is the true work of the practice, the cream of Buddhist teaching.

When we first come to Buddhism, we can immediately experience mindful breathing and it make us feel better. There's a tendency to grasp hold of this and think, "If I can breathe, if I can smile, if I'm able to follow my breathing when I feel a bit angry, then that's enough already." This kind of thinking stops us from going deeply into the deep teaching of non-discrimination that brings us to fearlessness, to the insight that helps us break through all our fetters. That is the greatest gift and the greatest fruit of the practice. If we're caught in ideas, caught in sorrow, caught in the way other people treat us, then that is a terrible waste of our lives.

The teachings on Right View and Dependent Co-arising offer us guidance on how to be with others. When we look deeply into others, we are looking deeply into ourselves at the same time. If we think the other person is someone other than us, that his or her success or failure has nothing to do with us, then we have not been successful in our looking deeply. The happiness of that person is linked to our own happiness. If we're not happy, the other person can't be happy, and our larger community will not be happy.

The insight generated from our understanding of the Sutra on the Middle Way can dissolve habit energy and generate the energies of great insight, love, and compassion. These energies can liberate us from suffering and help us to hand on to the future generations enough insight and love to release them from suffering like ours. We have to learn to live in happiness in the present moment. Every moment we walk in the present moment is a moment of liberation. Every step like this can liberate us and liberate countless generations of ancestors and descendants. With each step we walk with the Buddha.

Parallax Press, a nonprofit organization, publishes books on engaged Buddhism and the practice of mindfulness by Thich Nhat Hanh and other authors. All of Thich Nhat Hanh's work is available at our online store and in our free catalog. For a copy of the catalog, please contact:

PARALLAX PRESS
P.O. Box 7355
Berkeley, CA 94707
Tel: (510) 525-0101
www.parallax.org

BLUE CLIFF MONASTERY
3 Mindfulness Road
Pine Bush, NY 12566
www.bluecliffmonastery.org

DEER PARK MONASTERY
2499 Melru Lane
Escondido, CA 92026
www.deerparkmonastery.org

Monastics and laypeople practice the art of mindful living in the tradition of Thich Nhat Hanh at retreat communities in France and the United States. To reach any of these communities, or for information about individuals and families joining for a practice period, please contact:

PLUM VILLAGE
13 Martineau
33580 Dieulivol, France
www.plumvillage.org

The Mindfulness Bell, a journal of the art of mindful living in the tradition of Thich Nhat Hanh, is published three times a year by Plum Village. To subscribe or to see the worldwide directory of Sanghas, visit www.mindfulnessbell.org

RELATED TITLES BY THICH NHAT HANH

FROM PARALLAX PRESS

Breathe, You Are Alive!: Sutra on the Full Awareness of Breathing

Chanting from the Heart: Buddhist Ceremonies and Daily Practices

Peaceful Action, Open Heart: Lessons from the Lotus Sutra

The Diamond That Cuts Through Illusion: Commentaries on the Prajnaparamita Diamond Sutra

The Heart of Understanding: Commentaries on the Prajnaparamita Heart Sutra

Our Appointment with Life: The Budhha's Teaching on Living in the Present

Thundering Silence: Sutra on Knowing the Better Way to Catch a Snake

Touching the Earth: 46 Guided Meditations for Mindfulness Practice

Transformation and Healing: Sutra on the Four Establishments of Mindfulness

Two Treasures: Buddhist Teachings on Awakening and True Happiness

PARALLAX PRESS DONORS

Andre Brouwers

Renee Burgard

Alex Cline

Robin Costanzo: In memory of Wendy Robin Costanzo.

Leonard de Mol van Otterloo

Chip and Relma Hargus

Maurice Hoover: For the benefit of all beings. In the name of Pat Webb. In memory of David McCleskey, True Mountain of Goodness.

Tan Voong Seong: To benefit the work of Parallax Press. In memory of Leong Mee Yong.

Mozelle Sturlangson

Trish Thompson